PICTUREPEDIA

NOTE TO PARENTS

This book is part of PICTUREPEDIA, a completely
new kind of information series for children.
Its unique combination of pictures and words
encourages children to use their eyes to discover and
explore the world, while introducing them to a wealth
of basic knowledge. Clear, straightforward text
explains each picture thoroughly and provides
additional information about the topic.

'Looking it up' becomes an easy task with
PICTUREPEDIA, an ideal first reference for all types of
schoolwork. Because PICTUREPEDIA is also entertaining,
children will enjoy reading its words and looking
at its pictures over and over again. You can encourage and
stimulate further inquiry by helping your child
pose simple questions for the whole family to
'look up' and answer together.

PLANTS

A DORLING KINDERSLEY BOOK
Conceived, edited and designed by DK Direct Limited

Consultant Dr Richard Walker

Editors Anne de Verteuil, Val Burton

Art Editor Liz Black
Designer Tuong Nguyen

Series Editor Sarah Phillips
Series Art Editor Paul Wilkinson

Picture Researcher Anna Lord

Production Manager Ian Paton
Production Assistant Harriet Maxwell

Editorial Director Jonathan Reed
Design Director Ed Day

First published in Great Britain in 1993
by Dorling Kindersley Limited
9 Henrietta Street
London WC2E 8PS

A CIP catalogue record for this
book is available from the British Library.

ISBN 0-7513-5085-0

Reproduced by Colourscan, Singapore
Printed and bound in Italy by Graphicom

PLANTS

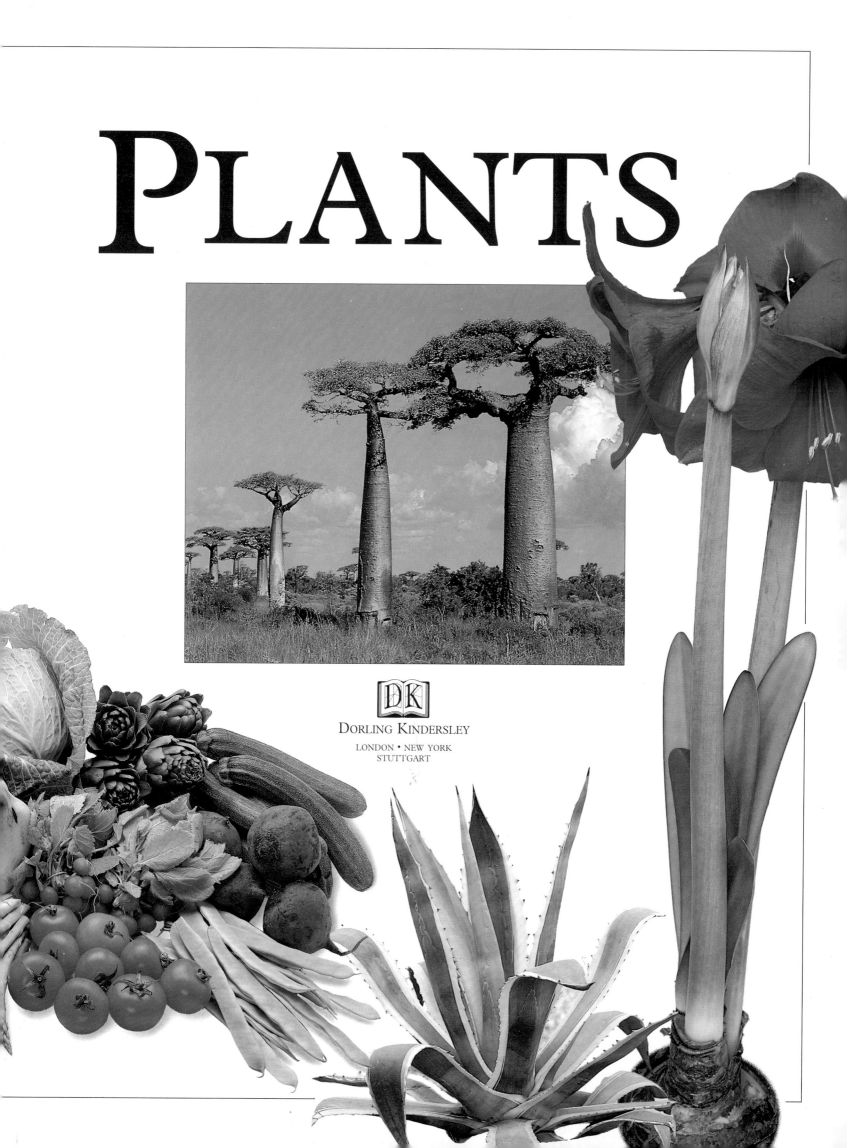

DK
DORLING KINDERSLEY
LONDON • NEW YORK
STUTTGART

CONTENTS

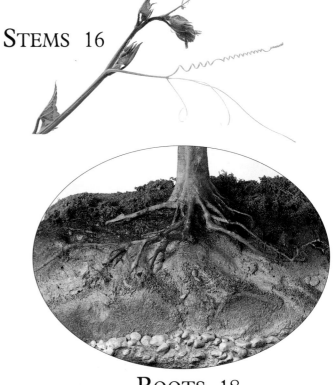

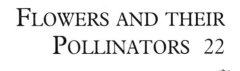

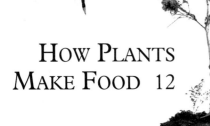

WHERE PLANTS GROW

Plants grow all over the world, from the icy Arctic to the steamy tropics. Anywhere in fact, where there is air, light and some water. Without plants our world would be a very different place. Plants provide us with food and hundreds of other useful things. Most important of all, they provide us with oxygen that we and all other living creatures need to breathe.

Arctic

North America

Silver Groves
Olive trees grow in warm southern European countries. Groves like this one bring us olive oil.

Green Mantle
Lush, green rainforests, like these in South America, grow where the climate is hot and wet.

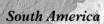

South America

Heat Lovers
Coconut palms grow only in places where it is hot and sunny all year round.

KEY

Arctic tundra	Desert
Coniferous forest	Deciduous forest
Tropical rainforest	Tropical deciduous forest
Scrubland	Mountains
Grassland	Ice

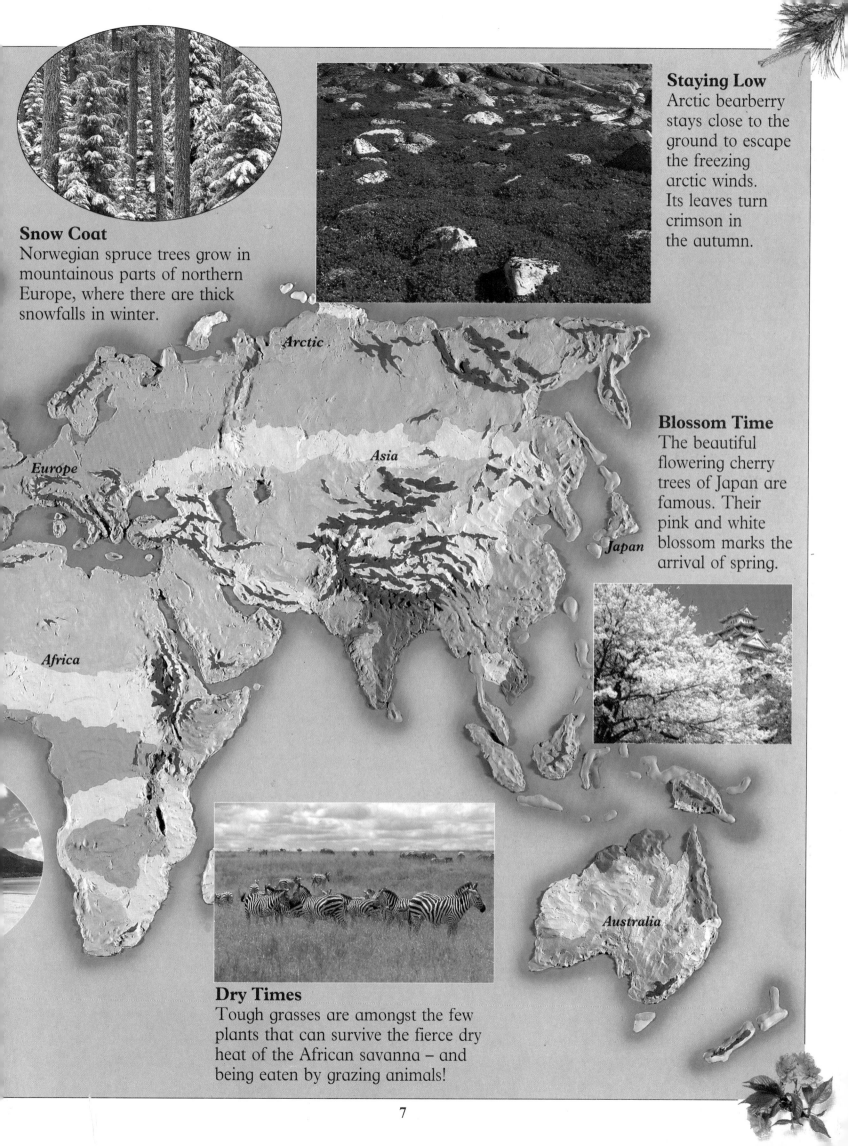

Snow Coat
Norwegian spruce trees grow in mountainous parts of northern Europe, where there are thick snowfalls in winter.

Staying Low
Arctic bearberry stays close to the ground to escape the freezing arctic winds. Its leaves turn crimson in the autumn.

Blossom Time
The beautiful flowering cherry trees of Japan are famous. Their pink and white blossom marks the arrival of spring.

Arctic

Europe

Asia

Japan

Africa

Australia

Dry Times
Tough grasses are amongst the few plants that can survive the fierce dry heat of the African savanna – and being eaten by grazing animals!

WHAT IS A PLANT?

The leaves are used for making food.

An apple tree and a cactus do not look much like each other. But they have more in common than you might think. They are both plants. Like all other plants they make their own food, and during the course of their lifetime, they can produce many new plants. To do these things they use their roots, stems, leaves and flowers. You will find that no matter how different one plant may look from another, each one is using these parts in much the same way, in order to live and grow.

Look, no Hands
Some plants do not need soil, they prefer to perch in trees. A stag's horn fern gets a good grip by wrapping its large fronds around a branch.

Trees have a main stem and many branches.

Apples contain seeds.

Hitching a Lift
Some plants use other plants for support. This passion flower can travel long distances by twining itself round the trunks and branches of trees.

The flowers make seeds for new plants.

The flexible stems can bend and twine.

Fresh Fruit
Apple trees are not best known for their flowers. But if they did not have flowers first, we would not have apples to eat.

Good Fronds
Fern leaves are called fronds and they grow straight out of the ground. Their stems are beneath the soil.

Feather Duster
Pampas grass has long sharp leaves, and those feathery plumes are its flowers.

This flower bud will open into a flower.

Don't Touch!
This cactus has a stem with branches but where are its leaves? The prickles are really special leaves.

Eyecatching
You can't miss these flowers. Like other plants that flower, orchids want to make quite sure that insects come visiting. So they advertise themselves with colours and scents that are attractive to insects.

Non-Flowering Plants
Most plants flower, but not all. Ferns, mosses, liverworts and lichens don't. The earliest plants to colonize the earth – over 300 million years ago – were non-flowering. These plants are their descendants. Instead of seeds, they produce tiny spores which become new plants.

Liverwort

Lichen

Moss

The curling tendrils hang on tight.

LEAVES

Leaves work very hard for plants. They make food and they also help plants to cope with serious problems like how to survive the cold, or get enough water. Leaves come in all sorts of shapes and sizes – large and small, thick and thin. In fact, you can tell quite a lot about a plant and where it grows, just by looking at its leaves.

Weatherproof

Scots pine trees need to be tough to survive long, cold winters. They have thousands of tiny, needle-like leaves. The needles have a waterproof coating to protect them from rain and snow.

Wind blows through the needles without damaging them.

Water Store

Agave plants grow in hot places where it may not rain for weeks on end. They are able to store water in their large thick leaves.

Their leaves can grow up to two metres long.

Open Sesame

Leaves have tiny holes called stomata, which the plant can open and close. When the stomata are open, they let air in and out, and water out. When they are closed, water can't escape from the leaves.

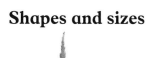

Shapes and sizes

Japanese maple

Himalayan birch

Fig

Acacia

Horse chestnut

Drip-Dry

Life in a tropical forest is hot and damp and there is no shortage of water. Monstera leaves have a special waxy surface, so the water can run off.

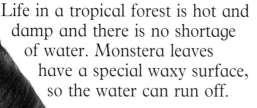

Monstera plants grow in the shade of trees that constantly drip moisture.

Prickly Customers

Plants can't run away from hungry animals, so they have to protect themselves. Prickly holly gets left alone!

Tough, glossy leaves are a good defence against wind and weather.

Shady Character

The maidenhair fern lives in damp, shady places, where its fragile leaves won't dry out in the Sun.

Water Signals

Leaves can't talk, but they can sometimes send a message. The leaves of this cyclamen are limp and drooping as if the plant is unhappy. The soil in the pot is dry, and the message is, 'Water Me'.

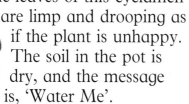

Do Plants Sweat?

Plants are constantly losing water through their leaves as part of a process called transpiration. Most of the time you can't see it happening. But if you put a plant inside a plastic bag and fasten it, after a while you will see water drops on the inside of the bag. The moisture you can see is coming from the leaves of the plant.

HOW PLANTS MAKE FOOD

Hungry animals can go out hunting for their food – but plants cannot. Instead, they make their own food in their leaves, using light from the Sun, water from the soil and carbon dioxide from the air. A plant's way of making food is called photosynthesis. It takes place during the day when the leaves are absorbing sunlight.

Reach for the Sun
These palms grow in the shade of tall trees. Their leaves are arranged like fans to help them catch all the light they can.

Colourful Cover-up
All leaves contain green chlorophyll. But in some leaves the green is hidden from sight by other, stronger colours.

The leaves of all plants contain a special pigment that gives them their green colour. It is called chlorophyll.

The roots take up water from the soil. It is drawn up the stem to the leaves.

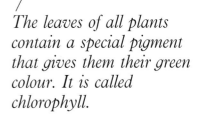

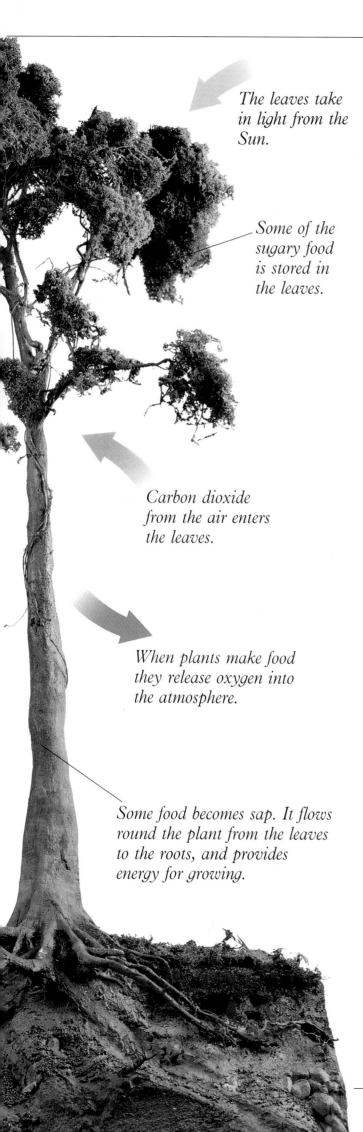

The leaves take in light from the Sun.

Some of the sugary food is stored in the leaves.

Carbon dioxide from the air enters the leaves.

When plants make food they release oxygen into the atmosphere.

Some food becomes sap. It flows round the plant from the leaves to the roots, and provides energy for growing.

Rest Time
Without sunlight, plants cannot make food. When it is dark they shut down for the night by closing their stomata.

Photosynthesis
Chlorophyll in the leaves absorbs sunlight. Sunlight provides the plant with energy to turn water and carbon dioxide into food.

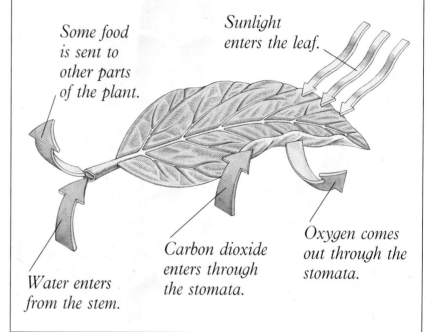

Some food is sent to other parts of the plant.

Sunlight enters the leaf.

Water enters from the stem.

Carbon dioxide enters through the stomata.

Oxygen comes out through the stomata.

Bare tree in winter

Tree in summer leaf

Hibernation
In winter there is less light and the water often freezes in the ground. It is difficult to make food, so plants grow very little at this time of year. Many trees shed their leaves.

CARNIVOROUS PLANTS

Water Jugs
A pitcher plant has several pitchers, so it can catch a lot of flies.

Watch out! These plants are meat-eaters and they have some very cunning devices for trapping their victims. Unlucky insects, attracted by the plant's scent and colour, discover too late that they have been tricked. It is a nasty end for an insect, but a ready-made, nutritious meal for the plant.

The lid can close to keep rainwater out.

Gruesome Gruel
Flies lose their footing on the slippery rim of the hanging pitcher plant and tumble into the water below. They gradually dissolve into a kind of fly broth.

Rim with nectar

Venus Flytrap
The instant an unsuspecting insect lands, the Venus flytrap snaps into action.

To a fly, this pad looks like a safe landing place.

Pitcher for collecting water

Swamped
Most carnivorous plants, like these cobra lilies, grow in boggy places where the minerals they need are in short supply. The insects they catch make a vital addition to their diet, because they are rich in the missing minerals.

Remains of flies

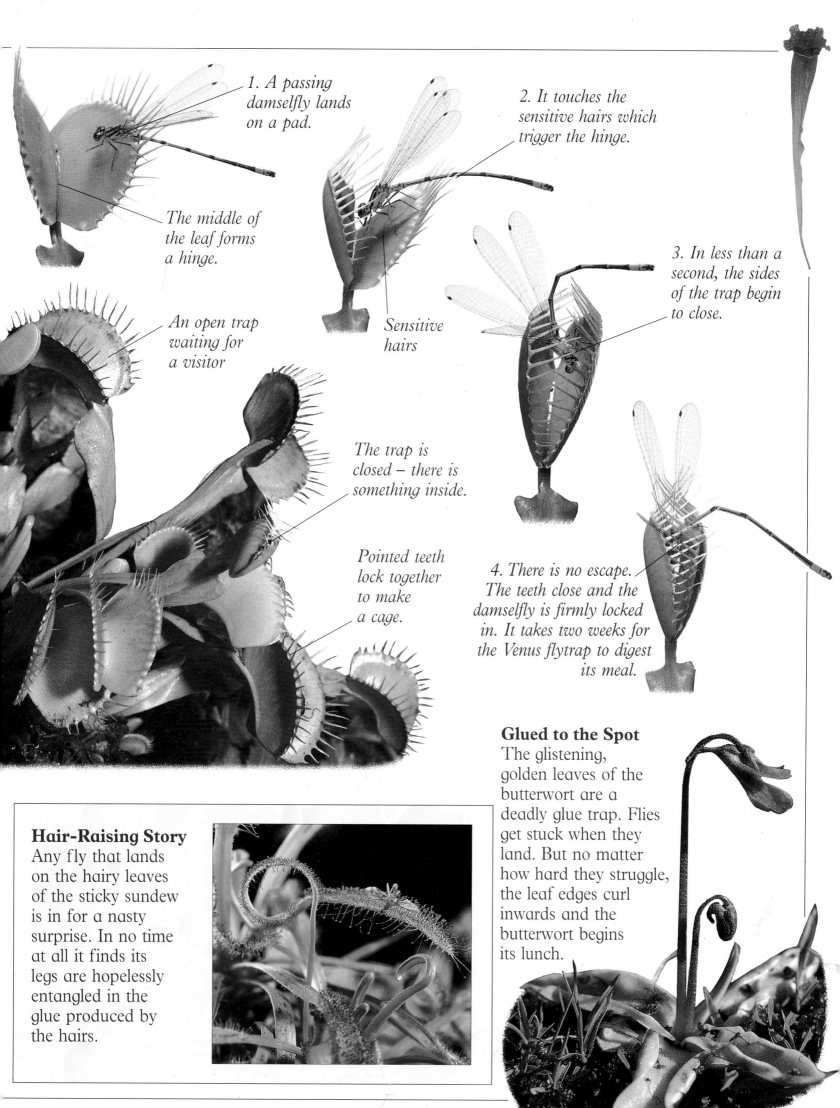

1. A passing damselfly lands on a pad.

The middle of the leaf forms a hinge.

2. It touches the sensitive hairs which trigger the hinge.

Sensitive hairs

3. In less than a second, the sides of the trap begin to close.

An open trap waiting for a visitor

The trap is closed – there is something inside.

Pointed teeth lock together to make a cage.

4. There is no escape. The teeth close and the damselfly is firmly locked in. It takes two weeks for the Venus flytrap to digest its meal.

Hair-Raising Story
Any fly that lands on the hairy leaves of the sticky sundew is in for a nasty surprise. In no time at all it finds its legs are hopelessly entangled in the glue produced by the hairs.

Glued to the Spot
The glistening, golden leaves of the butterwort are a deadly glue trap. Flies get stuck when they land. But no matter how hard they struggle, the leaf edges curl inwards and the butterwort begins its lunch.

STEMS

Roots, shoots, leaves and flowers are all connected to the plant's stem. Although it may not always stand as straight, the stem is rather like your backbone, holding all the different parts together. Being in the centre of everything means it is in the perfect position to carry water and food to every part of the plant.

Clever Creature
This aphid knows just where to go for food supplies! It takes less than a second to pierce the soft part of the stem which is full of nutritious sap.

This young tree is two years old.

Branches grow out from the stem and hold the leaves out to the light.

Sun Worshippers
The stems of sunflowers turn so their flowers can always face the sun.

As the tree gets older and taller, the main stem will thicken to form a trunk.

Clinging On
In its rush to the light, the sweet pea has no time to grow strong stems. Instead it uses twirling tendrils to wrap around other plants. They will support its fast climb to the top.

The Widest Spread on Earth
Just one banyan tree can make a forest! Their branches throw down special aerial roots. These grow into the ground and expand into trunks. A single tree in Calcutta has over 1,000 of these trunk lookalikes.

Water and minerals travel up the stem from the roots.

Supporting Role

The strong, hard stems of bamboo are called canes. In some parts of the world they make great thickets seven metres high.

Weak at the Knees

Gourd stems don't even attempt to stand up to support their fruit, which may weigh several kilos. They just trail gracefully over the ground.

The branches are slender and not yet very strong.

The inside of a bamboo cane is hollow.

Food is made in the leaves and travels down to the roots.

Keep Off !

It is quite difficult to get near a thistle but any animal that does, won't be back for a second bite.

Close-up of thistle stem

Section through cactus

Water Diet

African baobab trees have a special way of surviving. During the rainy season their trunks store so much water that they visibly swell up. These reserves get them through the hot, dry times, when their slimmer shape slowly returns.

Conservation

Desert cacti hold water reserves in their thick stems. Thirsty animals know that. But the barricade of fierce spines means no free drinks.

ROOTS

Roots are not pretty or colourful like leaves and flowers, but plants couldn't do without them! Anchored in the soil, they hold plants upright against wind and weather. They also grow out and down in search of water and minerals which are drawn all the way up to the leaves. Think how tall a tree can grow, and you can see it needs strong roots to keep it supported.

There are little pockets of air in the soil. Without air, roots would wither and die.

Roots can fit themselves into tiny spaces.

When earthworms burrow they help to add air to the soil.

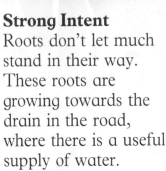

The roots of the tree grow outwards to balance the spread of the branches above.

Knobbly Knees
Swamp cypresses grow in boggy ground, where there is not enough air. These strange bumps probably supply the roots with the air they need. They are known as cypress knees.

Strong Intent
Roots don't let much stand in their way. These roots are growing towards the drain in the road, where there is a useful supply of water.

Rootless Wonder
Draped like strange beards over the branches of trees, the extraordinary Spanish moss plant survives with no roots at all. Spanish moss grows in subtropical climates where the air is very wet. It absorbs all the moisture it needs through its fine, thread-like leaves.

Rock Climbers
Alpine plants grow against rock faces, to protect themselves from high winds and icy squalls. Their tiny roots wriggle into cracks in the rock.

Most roots grow in the top 30 centimetres of soil. This part contains most of the important minerals the tree needs.

Every root grows a mass of tiny hairs near its tip to absorb water from the soil.

Water Crops
Plants need water, minerals and some support for their roots. But they do not necessarily need soil. Today many food crops are grown entirely in water with special pebbles. They are given liquid minerals to replace those in the soil.

INSIDE A FLOWER

Hibiscus

When you look at flowers you notice many colours, shapes and sizes. Some plants have a single flower, others have so many it is impossible to keep count. But stop and take a closer look – this time inside. However different they may look, flowers all have the same basic parts. This is because all plants produce flowers for the same purpose: to make seeds so another plant can grow.

Lily

Each male anther produces masses of tiny pollen grains.

The female stigma is the part where insects leave pollen.

Mistaken Identity
You could be confused by this poinsettia. What look like bright red petals are actually a kind of leaf, called a bract. The real flowers are the tiny green dots in the centre.

Grand Finale
Not all plants flower every year, but there is no other plant which is as slow as the puya raimondii from South America. It takes 150 years to produce a massive flower spike, up to 10 metres tall. Exhausted, it then dies, but luckily, not before it has managed to produce a few seeds.

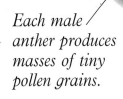

Mighty Magnolias

The last of the dinosaurs may have munched on magnolias like these. Magnolia trees are one of the oldest flowering plants. They have been around for one hundred million years, and they are still growing today.

The petals are brightly coloured, with special markings to attract insects.

Flower Arrangement

All these flowers have the same basic parts, but they are arranged on the stem in different ways.

These bell-shaped flowers hang down.

Each tiny point is a flower.

Is This a Flower?

Tropical orchids like this one often look more like strange insects than flowers.

Hundreds of small flowers grow in a single spike.

The flowers of the spider orchid can be up to 60 centimetres long.

Daisy petals are arranged like the rays of the Sun.

Each of these tightly packed flowers is called a floret.

Poppy petals open out to the light.

Snake's head fritillary

Allium

Mullein

Transvaal daisy

Poppy

Yarrow

FLOWERS AND THEIR POLLINATORS

Most plants cannot make seeds without some outside help. The first job is to move pollen from the male anther of one flower to the female stigma of another. This is called pollination. Plants cannot travel, but their flowers produce sweet nectar which animals love. As the animal feeds on the nectar, some pollen rubs onto its body. Each time it moves on to another flower, it leaves some pollen behind and picks up a new supply.

Honey Hunters
As it feasts on nectar, the Australian honey possum gets pollen on its fur.

Pollen Stop
Bees flit from flower to flower all day, feeding on nectar. Each time they stop, they pick up some pollen.

This bee is having a good pollen bath.

A flower, not a fly!

Clever Tricks
Fly orchids look and smell like the real thing. Male flies looking for a mate are easily tricked. They buzz off in disgust, taking the orchid's pollen with them.

Pollen from the anthers of the flower sticks to the butterfly's body.

Nectar Gatherers
Brightly coloured flowers attract butterflies looking for nectar.

Pollen Galore
Male catkin flowers dangle to catch the wind. They produce masses of pollen to make sure that some will be blown onto the stigmas of the female flowers.

Special Collection
When the hummingbird pushes its long beak deep inside the flower to collect the nectar, some pollen brushes off onto its body.

Inside Story
Not many insects would ever find the flowers of the fig tree. They actually grow inside the figs! They are pollinated by special fig wasps that live inside the fig. When the flowers are producing pollen, some of the wasps leave home. They move into another fig, carrying pollen with them on their bodies.

Pollen is brushed onto the bat's fur as it moves from flower to flower.

The bat's long tongue is perfect for whisking out the nectar.

On its nightly nectar hunt, one bat can pollinate several flowers.

Tropical Favourite
The bird of paradise flower grows in the tropics. It is pollinated by bats as well as by birds.

Bats find it easy to pick out the spiky shape of the bird of paradise flower at night.

FLOWERS BECOME FRUITS

After they have been pollinated, flowers produce seeds and fruits. The fruits protect the seeds and keep them safe until the time comes for them to grow. Like flowers, fruits come in all sorts of shapes and sizes. Horse chestnuts make conkers, dandelions make parachutes, and plum trees make plums. Every fruit has its own kind of seed. Some are light enough to be blown away on the wind, others are armour-plated so they can be swallowed by animals and pass out in their droppings without being damaged!

1. The swelling beneath the flower is called the receptacle and it will become the fruit.

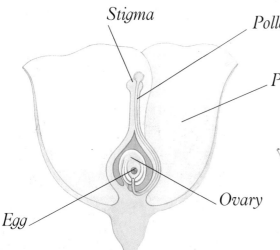

Stigma

Pollen grain tube

Petal

Ovary

Egg

Fertilization

An insect leaves some pollen on the stigma of a flower, and fertilization can take place. Each tiny pollen grain grows a long tube. The tube grows down until it reaches the ovary where eggs are produced. Now a male gamete from the pollen tube joins with an egg from the ovary, and a seed is born.

Leaving Home

Seeds need space and light to grow. If they fall straight off the parent plant, they have to struggle to grow in its shadow. So plants use all sorts of clever devices for making sure their seeds are carried away from them by wind or animals. Some have exploding pods that catapult the seeds into the air.

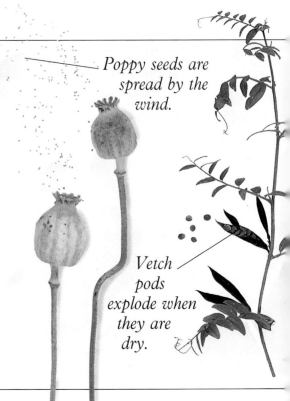

Poppy seeds are spread by the wind.

Vetch pods explode when they are dry.

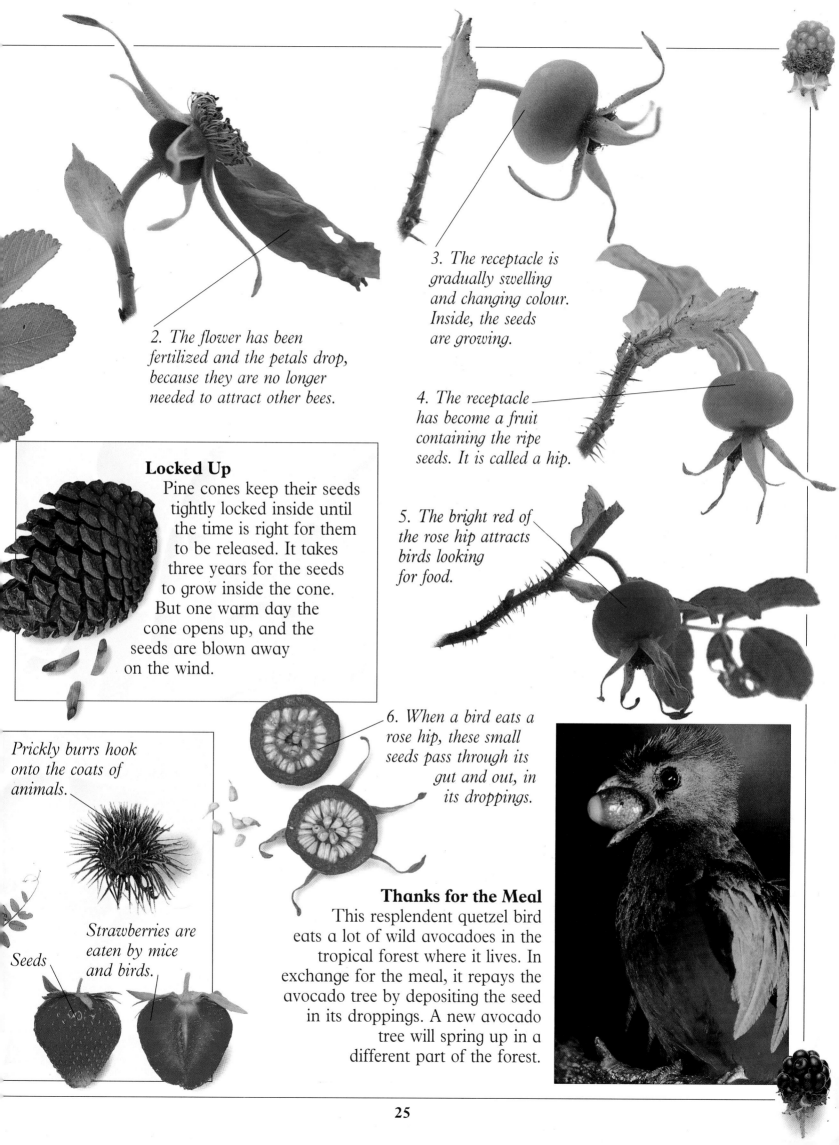

2. The flower has been fertilized and the petals drop, because they are no longer needed to attract other bees.

3. The receptacle is gradually swelling and changing colour. Inside, the seeds are growing.

4. The receptacle has become a fruit containing the ripe seeds. It is called a hip.

5. The bright red of the rose hip attracts birds looking for food.

Locked Up
Pine cones keep their seeds tightly locked inside until the time is right for them to be released. It takes three years for the seeds to grow inside the cone. But one warm day the cone opens up, and the seeds are blown away on the wind.

6. When a bird eats a rose hip, these small seeds pass through its gut and out, in its droppings.

Prickly burrs hook onto the coats of animals.

Strawberries are eaten by mice and birds.

Seeds

Thanks for the Meal
This resplendent quetzel bird eats a lot of wild avocadoes in the tropical forest where it lives. In exchange for the meal, it repays the avocado tree by depositing the seed in its droppings. A new avocado tree will spring up in a different part of the forest.

SEEDS BECOME PLANTS

Below ground, a seed is waiting to start life. But until it gets the right signals, a seed will remain just a seed. As soon as the soil becomes warm and damp the seed can begin to absorb moisture. This makes it swell and the seedcase splits open. Germination has begun – and the seedling starts to grow towards the light.

Wall Flowers
Some seeds land in odd places – and there they grow!

The leaves unfold into a fan shape.

Peanuts

Peanut bush

Coffee bush

Coffee beans

Seed and Plant
You may recognize these seeds, but do you know what they grow into?

Oak tree

Acorns

Lemon tree

Lemon pips

Roots grow down through the husk of the coconut.

Eggshells

Mustard and cress seeds

Damp cotton wool

On the Beach
A coconut can travel long distances by sea, until it is washed up onto the shore. In the warm sand, it sprouts and starts to grow.

Fast Food
Mustard and cress seeds are quick and easy to grow. Put some damp cotton wool in clean eggshells and sprinkle a few seeds on top. Look at the seeds each day and keep the cotton wool damp. In about ten days you will have your own home-grown salad!

Some Like it Hot
Some seeds must literally go through fire and water before they can germinate. In the arid Australian outback, fierce fires can rip across the land. They wake the dormant seeds of these acacia trees.

The stem is formed from the stalks of the leaves.

As the shoot gets longer and thicker, the first leaves open.

The coconut contains liquid, so the seedling has its own water supply for a while.

Inside the bean, you can see the part that is the future root.

A first sign of life – the root pushes through the skin of the bean.

The shoot appears above ground. This is the stem.

Roots and Shoots
When the soil gets warm in spring, this broad bean germinates and begins to grow.

GROWING WITHOUT SEEDS

Piggyback plant

Most flowering plants use their seeds to make new plants – but not all. Some plants can turn part of themselves into new plants, using their stems, their roots or their leaves. This is useful, because it means that they can spread themselves without any outside help from birds or insects. Some of these plants also use this method of reproduction to cover a lot of ground.

Leaf

Stem

Protective Parent
As the urn plant is flowering, new plants start to grow from the base of the plant. Gradually the parent plant withers away, but the young plants remain attached. By the time the parent plant has died, the young plants are ready to take its place.

One Potato, Two Potatoes
If we did not dig up sweet potatoes to eat, they would sprout, and become new plants with leaves and flowers. A sweet potato is a kind of swollen underground root called a tuber.

Tuber

New shoot

Roots

New growth starts here

Move Along
Ginger has a knobbly underground stem called a rhizome. The stem grows horizontally, sending up new shoots as it grows along.

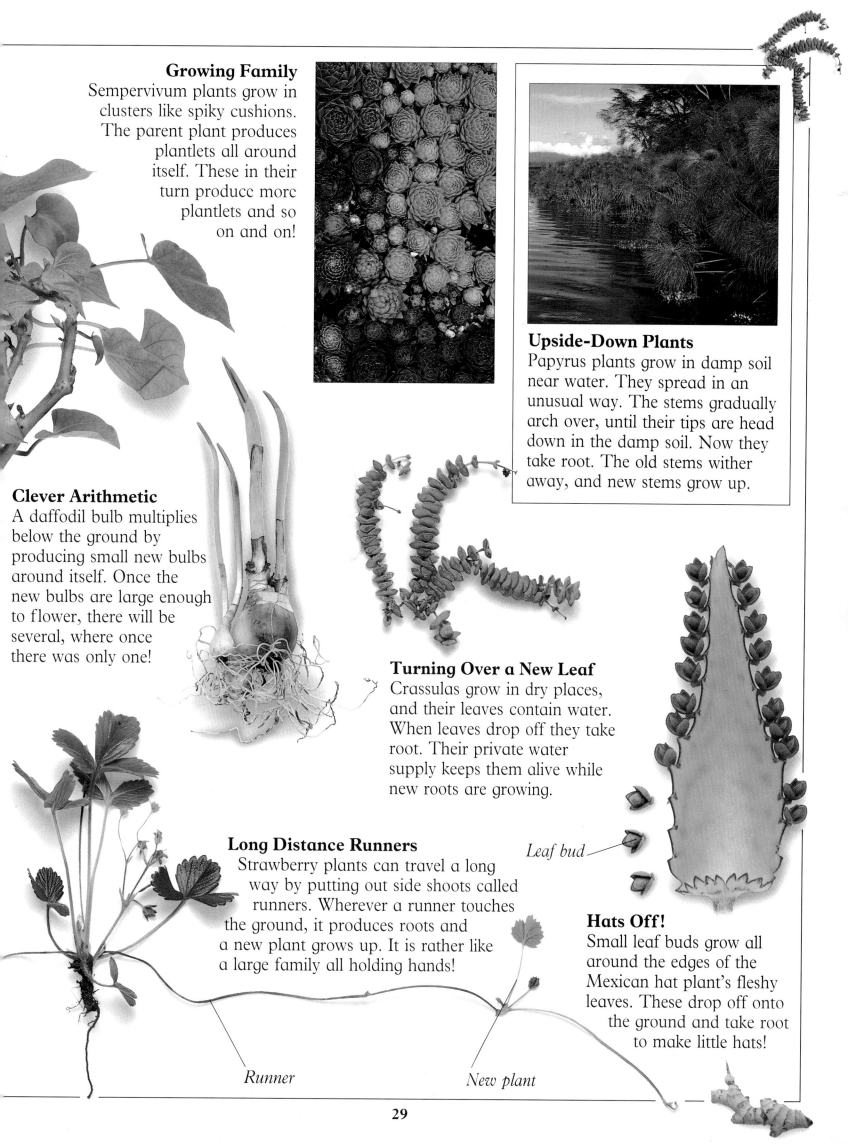

Growing Family

Sempervivum plants grow in clusters like spiky cushions. The parent plant produces plantlets all around itself. These in their turn produce more plantlets and so on and on!

Upside-Down Plants

Papyrus plants grow in damp soil near water. They spread in an unusual way. The stems gradually arch over, until their tips are head down in the damp soil. Now they take root. The old stems wither away, and new stems grow up.

Clever Arithmetic

A daffodil bulb multiplies below the ground by producing small new bulbs around itself. Once the new bulbs are large enough to flower, there will be several, where once there was only one!

Turning Over a New Leaf

Crassulas grow in dry places, and their leaves contain water. When leaves drop off they take root. Their private water supply keeps them alive while new roots are growing.

Leaf bud

Long Distance Runners

Strawberry plants can travel a long way by putting out side shoots called runners. Wherever a runner touches the ground, it produces roots and a new plant grows up. It is rather like a large family all holding hands!

Hats Off!

Small leaf buds grow all around the edges of the Mexican hat plant's fleshy leaves. These drop off onto the ground and take root to make little hats!

Runner

New plant

LIFE CYCLES

The flower bud opens out.

In winter the countryside looks bare. Trees and bushes remain, but many smaller plants disappear. This is because a lot of plants without woody stems are not able to survive the cold. But even though you cannot see them above ground in winter, these plants will reappear in spring. Some take a rest under ground. Others die, but before they do, they make seeds which will become new plants when spring arrives.

Each stem has four large flowers.

As the weeks go by the stem grows taller.

Super Store

An amaryllis can live for many years. By storing food and energy in its underground bulb, it can take a rest in winter. Plants that do this are called perennials.

A flower bud forms.

When the amaryllis has finished flowering, it keeps its leaves for a while. This means it can make food by photosynthesis and store the food in its bulb.

In winter when it is cold and dark, the bulb shows no signs of life.

When the soil becomes warm and damp, the roots begin to take up water.

As the days get warmer and lighter, green shoots push up from the bulb.

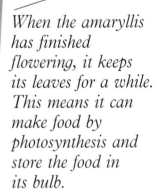

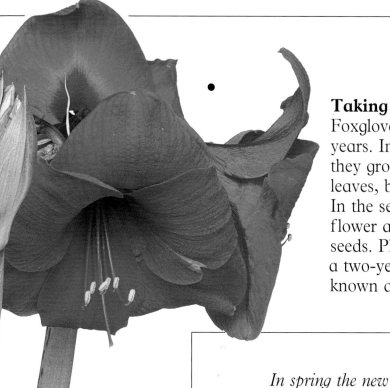

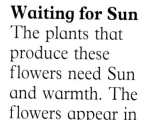

Taking Their Time

Foxgloves live for two years. In the first year they grow stems and leaves, but no flowers. In the second year, they flower and produce seeds. Plants which have a two-year life cycle are known as biennials.

Waiting for Sun

The plants that produce these flowers need Sun and warmth. The flowers appear in spring or summer.

Peony
(perennial)

In spring the new plant grows and prepares to flower.

Life Goes On

Some plants can't store food. Instead, they complete their whole life cycle before winter. These plants are called annuals. Before it dies, this nasturtium makes plenty of seeds. Over winter the seeds lie safely in the soil. When spring comes they germinate and start to grow.

In summer the plant flowers and produces seeds.

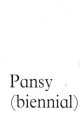

By autumn the seeds have been scattered, and the plant dies.

Tulip
(perennial bulb)

When winter approaches the leaves will die. The bulb can rest because it has stored food from the sunny days.

Agapanthus
(perennial)

Disappearing Trick

Not all perennials are bulbs. Other summer flowers, like this delphinium, store energy in their roots over the winter. In spring, Sun warming the soil gives the message for new shoots to push up through the ground.

Pansy
(biennial)

Sweet pea
(annual)

PLANTS TO EAT

We all rely on plants for our food and we eat an amazing variety of them. Some are easy to recognize, but there are lots of others which have been specially processed and mixed together before they are used. This means that by the time the plant arrives on your plate you often have to think quite hard before deciding what it is!

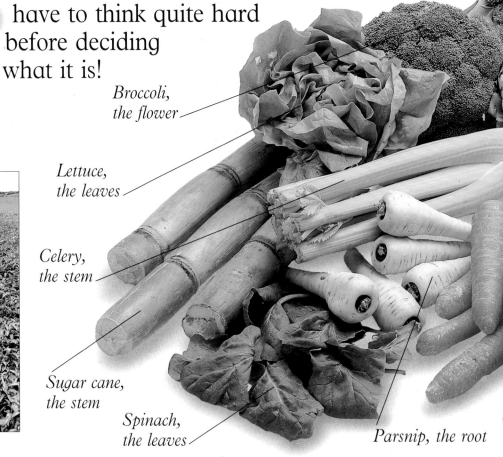

Broccoli, the flower

Lettuce, the leaves

Celery, the stem

Sugar cane, the stem

Spinach, the leaves

Parsnip, the root

Tutti Frutti
These delicious fruits come from countries where there is plenty of Sun and warmth to ripen them.

Tea plantation

Time for Tea
The tea that we drink is made from the leaves of the tea bush, which is grown in India, Sri Lanka and China. To make black tea the leaves are dried, crushed, fermented and dried again.

Delicious Plants
When you bite into a slice of scrumptious chocolate cake, you may not know it, but you are eating at least four different plants! Chocolate cake contains chocolate from cocoa pods, sugar from sugar cane, flour from wheat, and margarine from soya beans.

Root, Shoot or Fruit?

When you eat vegetables, do you know which part of the plant you are eating?

Cauliflower, the flower

Cabbage, the leaves

Artichoke, the flower bud

Miracle Bean

Some plants are particularly valuable as food crops, and one of these is the 'winged bean', which grows wild in New Guinea. Every single part of the plant can be eaten: leaves, flowers, and seed pod. The root tubers can be fried, roasted, boiled or baked. The mature seeds can be ground into flour, crushed for oil, and even made into a coffee-like drink. No wonder it is called the 'Supermarket on a Stalk'!

Courgettes (zucchini), the fruit

Good Taste

Herbs and spices are used to add flavour to our food. They come from all over the world.

Bayleaf – from Europe

Mustard – seed, from Europe

Cinnamon – tree bark, from Sri Lanka

Banana, the fruit

Radish, the root

Beetroot, the root

Cloves – flower buds, from Zanzibar

Asparagus, the stem and leaves

Tomatoes, the fruit

Runner beans, the fruit

Carrot, the root

Ginger – underground stem, from Jamaica

Rape seeds

Olives

Odd one Out!

Most oil comes from seeds but olive oil is made from the fruit of the olive tree.

Peanuts

Soya beans

Sunflower seeds

Sesame seeds

USEFUL PLANTS

Wood pulp is added to toothpaste to make it easy to squeeze onto the toothbrush!

Every day, from the moment we get up and brush our teeth until the last bedtime story, we are using things made from plants. Plants provide us with fuel, shelter, clothing, medicines and much, much more. In fact, the plant life of the world is so rich and varied, that scientists are constantly discovering new plants and new ways of using them.

Some plant fertilizers are made from seaweed.

This hat is made from palm leaves.

Many shampoos contain coconut oil.

Soap contains vegetable oils.

Loofahs are a kind of dried gourd.

Rubber comes from the bark of the rubber tree. The bark is punctured to let the liquid rubber flow out.

Wax from palm trees is used in wax furniture polish.

The fibres of the cotton plant are used to make cotton clothes.

Cotton thread

This doormat is made from coconut fibre.

Cotton wool balls

Plant Power
When sugar cane is fermented, it makes alcohol. In some countries it is used as a substitute for petrol. In Brazil, nearly one quarter of the cars are run on Alcool.

Jute
The stringy stems of jute are woven into sacks, ropes, carpets and the soles of shoes.

Black Wattle
The pulp of this plant is moulded to make toothbrushes, combs, buttons and even paper.

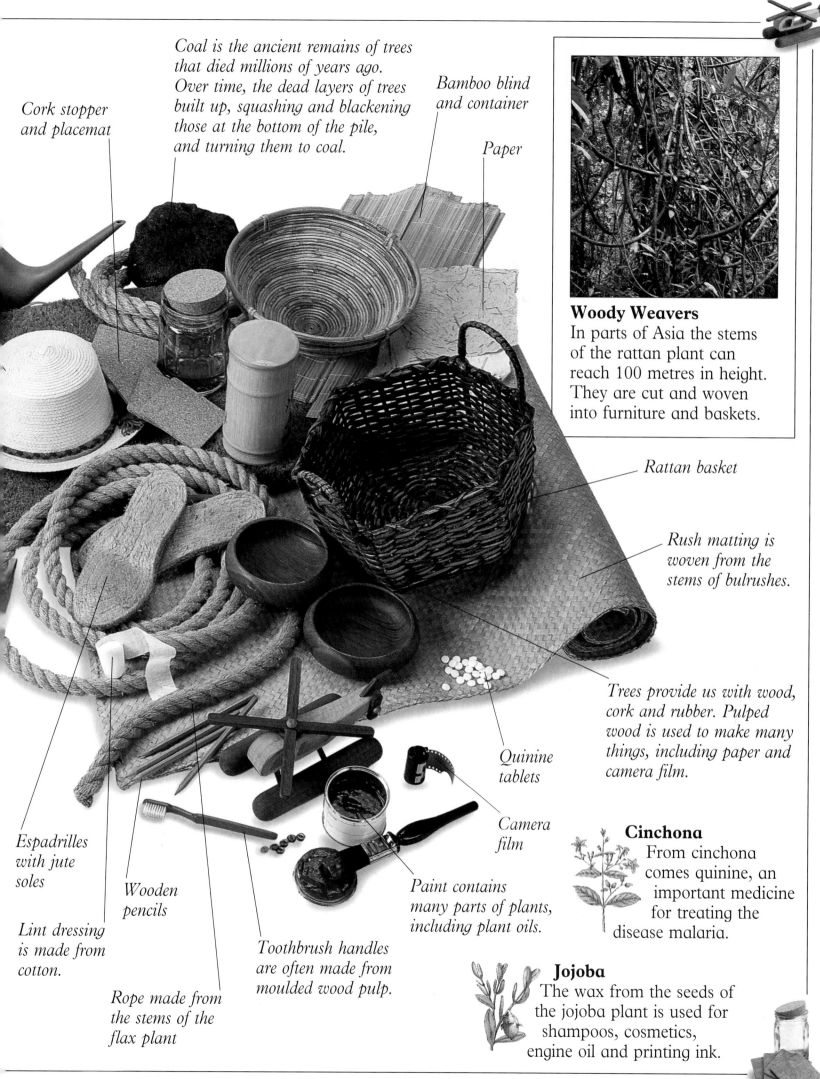

Cork stopper and placemat

Coal is the ancient remains of trees that died millions of years ago. Over time, the dead layers of trees built up, squashing and blackening those at the bottom of the pile, and turning them to coal.

Bamboo blind and container

Paper

Woody Weavers
In parts of Asia the stems of the rattan plant can reach 100 metres in height. They are cut and woven into furniture and baskets.

Rattan basket

Rush matting is woven from the stems of bulrushes.

Trees provide us with wood, cork and rubber. Pulped wood is used to make many things, including paper and camera film.

Espadrilles with jute soles

Wooden pencils

Lint dressing is made from cotton.

Rope made from the stems of the flax plant

Toothbrush handles are often made from moulded wood pulp.

Quinine tablets

Paint contains many parts of plants, including plant oils.

Camera film

Cinchona
From cinchona comes quinine, an important medicine for treating the disease malaria.

Jojoba
The wax from the seeds of the jojoba plant is used for shampoos, cosmetics, engine oil and printing ink.

TREES

Trees are the longest living of all plants. They grow strong, woody trunks so that they can tower above other plants and get plenty of light. There are trees that lose all their leaves in one go when the weather gets cold. They are known as deciduous trees. Others are evergreen and shed a few leaves at a time throughout the year.

Monkey puzzle tree

Bark is very important. It protects all the living, working parts of the trunk.

This part of the trunk is still alive and busy, carrying water and food to the rest of the tree.

Fiery Finale
Before they fall, the leaves of many deciduous trees change colour. The green chlorophyll disappears, revealing other colours that were hidden. Chemicals in the leaves deepen these colours to fiery golds and reds.

Silver birch

Bark
As trees grow, their trunks expand. The bark cracks to make lots of different patterns.

Paperbark maple

Tibetan cherry

Holding Fast
Over the years, wind has shaped and battered the branches of this tree. But its trunk and strong roots keep it standing.

Deciduous trees

Spanish oak

American mountain ash

Weeping willow

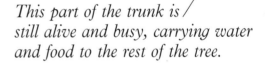

36

Cross Section

Every year a tree adds a new layer of growth to its trunk and branches. Look at this slice from a tree's trunk, and you will see lots of rings. Each ring shows the growth made by the tree in one year. By counting the rings you can tell how old a tree is.

A wide ring shows that the tree grew a lot in this year.

A bad year for growth! Thin rings show how slowly trees can sometimes grow.

Shagbark hickory

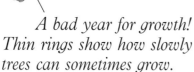

Snake-bark maple

Cork oak

Evergreen trees

Deodar

Mountain gum

Black spruce

The Incredible Hulk

What size waist do you have? The trunk of this giant redwood in California measures 24 metres all the way round, and stands over 83 metres high. It is so famous it has even been given a name – General Sherman!

WOODLAND PLANTS

Skeleton leaves

There is more to a wood than just trees! Very often a whole community of other plants and animals live and grow in its shelter. All these living things, down to the smallest earthworm, have a part to play in the life of a wood. The plants provide the animals with food, and the animals help new plants to grow by spreading their seeds.

A Year in the Life of a Wood
These beech trees are growing at the edge of a wood. Year after year, they grow and change with the seasons.

Frond unrolling

First to Flower
In early spring, pale primroses nestle close to the ground.

Spring
Sunlight comes in through the new leaves of the beeches. Woodland plants, like bluebells, flower in spring while there is enough light under the trees.

Waking Up
Fern fronds seem to be stretching themselves after their winter sleep. From tight green knobs on the ground, they gradually unroll until they are fully open.

Summer
The beeches are in full leaf and they cast shade onto the ground beneath them. Bracken doesn't mind shade, and often grows around trees.

Beech Banquet

Beech seeds are called nuts or masts. Some will be eaten by birds and squirrels. Some will grow into new beech trees.

Winter

The branches are bare and snow covers the ground. Smaller plants have died or disappeared below ground, and the trees themselves have stopped growing. Yet in just a few weeks' time, life will begin to stir again.

Lonesome Pines

In this evergreen pine wood there is not much variety. A thick layer of pine needles builds up on the ground and not many plants can grow. This, in turn, means fewer animals will make their homes here.

Autumn

In autumn, the nights are colder and there is less sunlight. This is the signal for many plants to shed their leaves in preparation for the cold weather ahead. But before they fall, the leaves of the beeches turn golden yellow.

Super Soil

Beneath the trees the earth is rich. As fallen leaves rot, they return minerals to the soil.

As dead wood decays it soaks up water.

Still Life

In a wood, everything is recycled, even trees. This fallen log has become a home for damp-loving mosses and ferns.

WATER PLANTS

Plants that grow in water do not need stiff stems to support them. Instead, they have trailing, flexible stems that can bend and sway with the movement of the water. Their leaves float on the surface – or just beneath it – so they can catch the light they need for photosynthesis. Their roots and stems are designed so that they can absorb minerals from the water, and some have no roots at all.

Spreading Out

Floating duckweeds can spread very quickly. Their tiny leaves are food for water insects, snails – and ducks!

The leaves are called pads. They have a waxy, waterproof coating on top, so water can run off.

Water lilies grow long stems so their leaves can float on the surface of the water.

The flowers open during the day, and close at night.

Water lilies are rooted in the mud at the bottom of the pond.

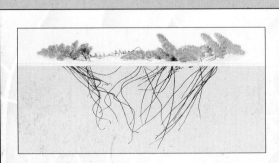

Fairy Fern

Miniature azolla is a water fern. Tiny hairs on its fronds trap air, and help to keep it afloat.

Floating Free

Not all water plants grow roots into the soil. This water hyacinth is free to float where it will. Its short, tangly roots absorb water and minerals as it moves around.

Reeds and grasses grow in the wet soil at the water's edge.

The roots grow together to help keep the muddy soil from slipping into the pond.

Floating Saucers

The giant water lily of the Amazon is the world's largest water plant. Pads can measure 1.5 metres across. They have strong ribs to keep them flat and rigid.

Star Turn

In summer, water soldier plants pop up to the surface to flower. When their flowers are over, they sink under the water again until next year.

Air Supply

Some plants live and grow entirely below water. They are very important to pond life. When they make food by photosynthesis, they release vital oxygen into the water.

DESERT PLANTS

Bunny-ears cactus

Deserts are places of extremes. Days are scorching hot, nights are often freezing. Sometimes it does not rain for years. The plants that grow here are built for survival. Many have long, spreading roots, waiting to collect any drop of rain when it falls. Most of them are able to store water in their stems, leaves or roots.

High above the ground on a tower of thorns, a hawk has found a safe place to nest.

The stem of the saguaro is pleated, and expands like a concertina to hold massive water supplies.

Plants lose water through their leaves, so cacti don't have any! Instead they have spines and a thick waxy skin to stop water from evaporating.

Desert Fruits
In the African desert, wild watermelons are an important source of water for people and animals.

Skyscraper
The tallest growing cactus is the giant saguaro. It towers over the deserts of south-western America, taking over two hundred years to reach 15 metres in height. One plant can weigh as much as two elephants. Three-quarters of this is water.

Imagine a Desert
Desert plants are easy to grow at home. They need a lot of light and very little water.

Resting Places
Wherever there is an underground water well or spring, the desert shoots into life. These shady islands of green in the desert sand are called oases.

Curious Cacti
Some cacti have strange shapes – and strange names too!

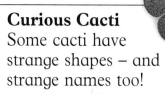

Cephalocereus senilis

Peek-a-boo!
Tiny baby-toes cacti live buried in hot sandy soil with only their tips peeping out.

The huge, brightly coloured flowers are bigger than the rest of the plant!

Plant or Pebble?
Animals don't eat stones – but they might if they realized that these pretty little pebbles were plants in disguise!

The stem tips have special windows which let light in.

Mammilaria elongata

Astrophytum myriostigma nudum

Race for Life
A quick downpour of rain and suddenly this desert is ablaze with colour. Many seeds which have been waiting below ground germinate in the sudden moisture.

Monvillea spegazzini

RAINFOREST PLANTS

Imagine you are walking through a steamy tropical rainforest. All around you leafy plants drip water. Tall trees rear up and disappear from sight. Their branches are covered with strange and beautiful plants, and creepers clamber up their trunks. Everywhere it is green, and hot, and very wet.

Tree-Dweller
Tree-dwelling orchids have dangling roots which absorb water from the damp air.

These trees grow closely together to make a dense canopy of leaves.

Private Pool
Urn plants collect water, and sometimes other things too! High up in the branches where the plant is perched, this tiny tree frog takes a bath.

Growing Everywhere
Rainforest trees are often laden with plants growing on their trunks and branches. Sometimes the weight is so great, whole branches crash to the ground. Plants that grow on trees are known as epiphytes.

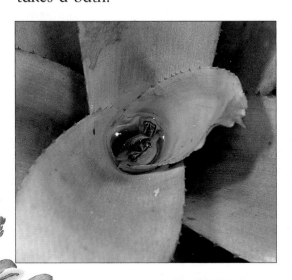

When a giant tree falls, light can enter from above. Plants and seedlings on the forest floor begin their race for the Sun.

The heads of these trees may be in blazing Sun, or in wet cloud.

A tree may grow five metres in a single year.

Rope-like liana stems snake up the tree trunks in search of light.

Colour Zone

These trees are the forest giants. Their brilliantly coloured flowers are a signal to butterflies and birds that there is nectar to be gathered and pollen to be spread!

Plant Paradise

Thousands of different plants grow in a rainforest. Many have great medical value. Some are so rare that they are not found growing anywhere else on Earth.

Gone Forever

Rainforests are the richest and most varied plant communities. But their existence is under threat from humans. Every year huge areas are burnt and cleared. Once the forest has gone, the soil rapidly becomes cracked and useless, and thousands of plants are lost forever.

AMAZING PLANTS

Plants are very good at making the best of a situation. Even in conditions that seem impossibly hot or cold, they carry on living and growing. You often find that the plants that grow in difficult places or live for long spans of time, have developed one special feature to help them survive. These great survivors may not all be great beauties, but they are certainly amazing plants!

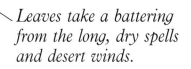

Leaves take a battering from the long, dry spells and desert winds.

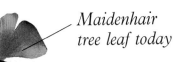

Maidenhair tree leaf today

This fossil leaf is over 200 million years old.

High Living
Air plants live on thin air! They use their roots to hang on to high mountain rocks or trees. They take all the water they need from the damp mists swirling round them.

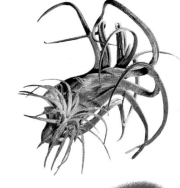

Unchanged
In the last 250 million years the Earth has changed dramatically. Ice ages have come and gone. But in all that time the maidenhair tree has hardly altered. It still has leaves just like its ancestors.

Bristlecone pines grow very, very slowly, often only a millimetre or two a year.

Truly Ancient
The amazing bristlecone pines are the oldest living things on Earth. The very oldest pine is a staggering 4,900 years old. That means it started life about 2907 BC.

The Never-Ending Story

Welwitschia plants grow only in one African desert. Each welwitschia produces only two leaves in its lifetime and it may live for 2,000 years. The longest and biggest leaves recorded were eight metres long and two metres wide.

Cone Carriers

Welwitschias produce cones which contain their seeds. Male and female cones are carried on separate plants. This one is a female plant.

Welwitschia leaves may look soft, but they are actually hard.

Tough Stuff

Some seeds must germinate as soon as they can, others are so tough they can lie around for hundreds of years. New plants have been grown from 1,000-year-old lotus seeds. Their seedcases were so hard, scientists had to dissolve them first with sulphuric acid.

Help from Humans

Research laboratories like this one at Kew Gardens in London, specialize in saving rare and endangered plants. Part of the plant's internal tissues or its seeds are grown inside a test tube, by a process called micro-propagation. When the plants are growing well, they will be replanted in the wild.

The leaves are brown and dry.

Who would guess this is the same plant!

Born Again

A good way of surviving long droughts is to play dead. The extraordinary resurrection plant can completely dry out for months on end. When the rains arrive it miraculously comes back to life.

GLOSSARY

Annuals Plants that live for just one year. During this time they grow from a seed, flower, make seeds and die.

Anther The male part of a flower which produces the pollen.

Biennials Plants that live for two years.

Bulb An underground foodstore, from which a new plant grows.

Carnivorous plants Plants that rely on insects and other small animals for food.

Carbon dioxide A colourless gas in the air which plants absorb to help them make food.

Chlorophyll The green colouring in plants which is needed to make food.

Cone Some trees, like conifers, do not have flowers. Instead they grow cones, which is where their seeds are made.

Deciduous plants Shrubs and trees that shed their leaves in autumn, and grow new ones in spring.

Epiphytes Plants that are not rooted in the ground. Instead they perch on the branches and stems of trees.

Evergreen plants Shrubs and trees that are continually losing and growing leaves, throughout the year.

Fertilization The joining together of a pollen grain and an egg to make a plant seed.

Fruit The casing which surrounds seeds until they are ready to start growing. It may be hard, like a nut, or soft like a plum.

Germination The growth from the seed of its first tiny shoot and root.

Minerals Substances found in the soil. They are only needed in tiny amounts, but they are vital for plants to grow well.

Nectar The sweet liquid inside flowers fed on by many insects and birds.

Ovary The female part of the flower which produces the eggs that are needed for making seeds.

Oxygen A gas that is released into the air by plants when they make food by a process known as photosynthesis.

Perennials Plants that live from year to year, like trees.

Photosynthesis The way plants make food, by using the energy from sunlight, together with water and carbon dioxide. The word photosynthesis means 'building with light'.

Pollen The fine powder produced by the anther inside a flower.

Pollination The movement of pollen from the male anther to the female stigma of a flower. It is necessary before seeds can be produced.

Reproduction The process of making new plants.

Sap The juice inside the stem of a plant. It consists of water and the sugary food made by plants in their leaves.

Seed The 'package of life' inside a fruit or cone, from which a new plant will grow.

Stigma The tip of the female part of the flower which receives the male pollen grains.

Stomata Tiny openings on the undersides of leaves.

Tendril A very fine stem on a climbing plant, which wraps itself around other plants for support.

Transpiration The movement of water up through the roots and stem of a plant, and out through its leaves.

Trunk The stem of a tree which has thickened over the years and developed hard wood.

Tuber A swollen underground stem and foodstore from which a new plant grows.

Acknowledgments

Photography: Peter Anderson, David Rudkin.

Additional Photography: Jane Burton, Peter Chadwick, Geoff Dan, Philip Dowell, Dave King, Andreas Einsiedel, Stephen Hayward, Jacqui Hurst, Trevor Melton, Andrew McRobb, Martin Norris, Kim Taylor, Matthew Ward, Steven Wooster.

Illustrations: Phil Weare, Michelle Ross (Linden Artists); Christine Robins (Garden Studios); Aziz Khan.

Models: Peter Griffiths.

Thanks to: Mark Lamey at Kew Gardens, Ray Waites at Wisley, Scallywags Child Model Agency, The Colour Company, Oxfam, Whittards of Chelsea and Caroline Brooke.

Index